I0008565

Python:

*Best Practices
to Programming Code
with Python*

Charlie Masterson

Table of Contents

professional before attempting any techniques outlined in this book.

By reading this document, the reader agrees that under no circumstances are is the author responsible for any losses, direct or indirect, which are incurred as a result of the use of information contained within this document, including, but not limited to, —errors, omissions, or inaccuracies.

Introduction

I want to thank you and congratulate you for reading the book, "Python: Best Practices for Programming Code with Python". This book contains proven steps and strategies on how to program in Python more effectively. When you first learn Python, you will be taught how to write code, but in many cases, you will not be taught how to write that code neatly.

If you speak to any Python programmer, ask them what it is they like about Python. I guarantee they will tell you that one of the main reasons is because it is easily readable. In fact, this is the absolute heart of the Python language, simply because computer code is read far more than it is written. Much of this is down to the fact that Python code follows a set of guidelines and "Pythonic" idioms – if you hear a programmer refer to a part of the code as not being "Pythonic", it means that it doesn't follow those guidelines and it doesn't express intent in any readable manner.

Code style and layout is incredibly important, as is consistency in the style that you use. With that said, there are times when consistency isn't the right thing and the guidelines are simply not applicable – you have to know when that time is and that is when best judgment comes into programming with Python.

With this guide, I am going to show you the absolute best way to write your code, tidying up your program and making it all more effective and efficient. I won't just give you the basic. I will delve deep into everything you need to know, from the layout of the code to how to write functions, idioms, and names.

I will talk about whitespaces and tabs, strings, and methods. I will also be giving you some general recommendations for Python programming along with the general concepts. In short, by the time you have read my Best Practice guide, you will be the best Python programmer you can possibly be.

My book does assume some prior knowledge of Python programming, so if you are a complete newbie to the programming scene, please familiarize yourself with Python code before you read this book. My aim is to help you to produce Python code that is free from, or at least has very few, complications or obvious problems, as well as making it more readable for others.

Thanks again for reading this book, I hope you enjoy it!

Chapter 1: General Concepts of Python Coding

Before we get properly into the book, these are the general concepts of coding that you should be aware of; concepts that will make life easier for you.

Explicit Code

While you can do all sorts of weird and wonderful things with Python, it is best to keep it straightforward and explicit.

A Bad Example:

```
def make_complex(*args):
    x, y = args
    return dict(**locals())
```

A Good Example:

```
def make_complex(x, y):
    return {'x': x, 'y': y}
```

Compare these examples; in the latter example of code, we explicitly received **x** and **y** from the caller and the return is an explicit dictionary.

The developer who wrote this knows what to do just by looking at the first line and the last line; this is not the case with the bad example.

One Line, One Statement

While there are compound statements, like the list comprehensions, that are allowed and, in many cases, appreciated, it is not good practice to have 2 statements that are disjointed on one code line.

A Bad Example:
```
print 'one'; print 'two'

if x == 1: print 'one'

if <complex comparison> and <other
complex comparison>:
    # do something
```

A Good Example:
```
print 'one'
print 'two'


if x == 1:
    print 'one'

cond1 = <complex comparison>
cond2 = <other complex comparison>
if cond1 and cond2:
    # do something
```

Returning Values

When you get a function that is ever-growing in complexity, it isn't unheard of to use several return statements in the body of the function. However, if you want to maintain clear intent and a good level of readability, you should try not to return values from several points in the function body.

When it comes to returning values within a function, there are 2 cases for doing so: the result that comes from a normally processed function return, and the errors that are indicative of incorrect input parameters or for any reason that the function cannot complete the computation.

If you don't want exceptions raised for the latter case, then it might be necessary for values, such as False or None to be returned, as an indication that the function was not able to perform properly. In cases such as this, it is best practice to return as soon as the wrong context has been noticed.

This will help to neaten up the function structure because all code that comes after the error return assumes that the condition has been met so that the main function result can be computed. As such, it is sometimes necessary to have several return statements like this.

That said, if a function contains several different courses it can go, it can be unwieldy to debug the result so it is preferable to maintain just one course. This also helps in working out code paths and, if you have several courses, it could be an indication that you need to re-look at your code and tidy it up.

For Example:

```
def complex_function(c, b, a):
    if not c:
        return None  # Raising an
exception might be better
    if not b:
        return None  # Raising an
exception might be better
    # Some elaborate code that is trying
to make x from c, b and a
    # Try not to return x if successful
    if not x:
        # A Plan-B calculation of x
    return x  # One exit point for the
value x will be helpful
                # when trying to maintain
the code.t
```

Chapter 2: Programming Recommendations

These are the basic recommendations for writing Python code, recommendations that you should follow if your code is going to be more effective and efficient as well as being readable.

- Your code must be written so that it doesn't disadvantage other Python implementations, such as **IronPython, Jython, PyPy, Psyco and Cython.**

For example, you should never rely on the efficient string concatenation of CPython that takes the form of `a=a+b` or `a+=b`. This is a somewhat fragile optimization, even though it super-efficient in CPython, because it won't work on al type sand it won't be present in any Python implementation that does not use refcounting.

Instead, where you use a part of the library that is performance-sensitive, you should use the `.join()` form instead. This will make sure that the concatenation is linear across all the different Python implementations.

- Never use an equality operator to make comparisons to a singleton such as None. Instead, use `is` or `not`.

You should also be wary of using `if x` when really you should be using `if is not None`. An example of this is when you are testing if an argument or a variable that defaults to a value of None was actually set to a different value. The other value could have a type that is false in the Boolean context.

- Rather than using the operator `not...is`, you should use `is not`. While they both are identical in terms of function, the first is low on the readability scale, making the second one more preferable. An example:

Use This:
```
if foo is not None:
```

Don't Use This:
```
if not foo is None
```

- When you implement an ordering operation with a rich comparison, you should implement all of the 6 operations instead of relying on some other code to exercise a comparison. Those operations are (`__eq__`, `__lt__`, `__ne__`, `__ge__`, `__gt__`, `__le__`)

To cut down on the effort needed, one particular decorator helps to generate any comparison methods that are missing. That decorator is `functools.total_ordering()`.

The style guidelines indicate that Python assumes reflexivity rules. As such, the Python interpreter might change things about by swapping `y > x` with `x < y`, or it may swap `y >= x` with `x <= y`.

You may also find that the argument `x ==` `y` has been swapped with `x != y`. The `min()` and `sort()` operations will also definitely use the `<` operator and the `max()` function will use the `>`operator. However, you should, as a best practice guide, use all of them so that there is no confusion.

- Rather than using an assignment statement that will bind a lambda expression to an identifier, use a `def` statement

A Good Example:
```
def f(x): return 2*x
```

A Bad Example:
```
f = lambda x: 2*x
```

The first example shows that the name given to the function object is 'f' rather than the collective <lambda>. This is the most useful for string representations and for tracebacks and, by using the assignment statement, you cut out the one benefit that a lambda expression offers over and above a def statement – that it may be embedded within a bigger statement.

When you want to derive exceptions, use Exception and not BaseException. Inheritance from the latter is reserved for those exceptions where it is pretty much always wrong to catch them

When you design your exception hierarchies, base them on the quality that is likely to be needed by catching exceptions, rather than on the location where the exception is raised. Always answer one question – "what has gone wrong?" rather than just saying that something is wrong. Use the conventions for class naming but do remember to add the "Error" suffix to the exception classes that produce an error.

There is no need to put any special suffixes on exceptions that are not errors and are used as flow-control or another form of signaling.

- When you use exception chaining, use it only where needed.

When you replace an inner exception deliberately, make sure that the right details are relocated into the newer exception. Examples of this are making sure the name of the attribute is preserved when you convert `KeyError` to `Attribute Error` or when you embed the original exception text into the message in the newer exception

- When using Python 2 and you raise an exception, always use the `raise ValueError)'message')` instead of `raise ValueError 'message'`

This is because the second example is neither valid nor legal syntax for Python 3. Also, the use of the containing parentheses means that there is no requirement to use continuation characters on a line when you add string formatting or when an exception argument is too long.

- When you catch exceptions, always mention specific ones wherever you can rather than using the bare except: clause

For Example:

```
try:
    import platform_specific_module
except ImportError:
    platform_specific_module = None
```

`KeyboardInterrupt` and `SystemExit` exceptions will be caught by a bare except: clause and this makes it much more difficult to interrupt programs using CTRL+C and they can also cover up other problems that may be there.

If you are looking to catch every exception that signals errors in the program, use except Exception:

A general rule is to only use the bare except: clause in one of these two cases:

1. If the traceback is being printed by the exception handler; that way, the user will be made aware of any errors

2. If cleanup work is needed but the code allows the exception to propagate up using raise. A more efficient way to do this would be to use `try...finally`.

When you are binding a caught exception to a name, use the explicit binding syntax from Python 2.6:

```
try:
    process_data()
except Exception as exc:
    raise
DataProcessingFailedError(str(exc))
```

This is the ONLY syntax that Python 3 supports and it cuts out any problems of ambiguity that are associated with the older-style syntax that is comma-based.

- When you are catching system errors, use the exception hierarchy from Python 3.3 rather than errno values. As well, when you use any try/except clause, try to limit the use of the try clause to the least amount of code. This will cut down the risk of errors being hidden

A Good Example:
```
try:
    value = collection[key]
except KeyError:
    return key_not_found(key)
else:
    return handle_value(value)
```

A Bad Example:
```
try:
    # Too broad!
    return handle_value(collection[key])
except KeyError:
    # Will catch a KeyError that is
raised by handle_value()
    return key_not_found(key)
```

- When you use a resource tool that is local to a specific code section, use it with a statement to make sure that it is cleaned immediately after use. You can also use a try/finally statement

- Always invoke a context manager through separate methods or functions whenever they are for a purpose other than getting and releasing resources.

A Good Example:
```
with conn.start_transaction():
    do_something_in_transaction(conn)
```

A Bad Example:

```
with conn:
    do_something_in_transaction(conn)
```

The second example does not give us any information that indicates whether the __enter__ and __exit__ methods do anything other than shutting the transaction. In this case, it is important to be explicit.

- Consistency in return statements is important. Either all of the function return statements or none of the return statements should return an expression or value. If a return statement does return an expression, any that do not return any value should state explicitly that the return is None and there should be a return statement at the end of that function

A Good Example:
```
def foo(x):
    if x >= 0:
        return math.sqrt(x)
    else:
        return None

def bar(x):
    if x < 0:
        return None
    return math.sqrt(x)
```

A Bad Example:
```
def foo(x):
```

```
    if x >= 0:
        return math.sqrt(x)

def bar(x):
    if x < 0:
        return
    return math.sqrt(x)
```

- Don't use string modules; use string methods instead

These are always faster and they share an API with the Unicode strings. This rule can be ignored if you need backward compatibility with a Python implementation that is earlier than 2.0

- Instead of using string slicing as a way of checking for suffixes and prefixes, use `".startswith()` and `".endswith()` instead

These are much cleaner methods and they are less prone to errors.

A Good Example:
```
if foo.beginswith('bar'):
```

A Bad Example:
```
if foo[:3] == 'bar':
```

- When you are comparing object types, use `isinstance()` instead of direct comparisons

A Good Example:
```
if isinstance(obj, int):
```

A Bad Example:
```
if type(obj) is type(1):
```

When you check to see if an object is actually a string, remember that it could be a Unicode string as well. In Python 2.0, Unicode and str share the base class called `basestring` so you could do:

```
if isinstance(obj, basestring):
```

However, in Python 3, you won't find basestring or Unicode, only str and bytes objects are not strings anymore, they are integer sequences instead.

For a sequence – tuples, lists, strings, etc. – make use of the fact that an empty sequence is false.

A Good Example:
```
if not seq:
    if seq:
```

A Bad Example:
```
if len(seq):
```

```
if not len(seq):
```

Don't include any string literals that require significant levels of trailing whitespace because this is not distinguishable and some text editors will remove them

Don't use == to compare a Boolean value to True or False:

A Good Example:
```
if greeting:
```

A Bad Example:
```
if the greeting == True:
```

An Even Worse Example:
```
if the greeting is True:
```

Chapter 3:
Code Layout

The most obvious place to start with is how to layout your code. I will be giving you the best practice guidelines for code layout along with examples on how to do it and how not to:

Indentation and Alignment

Every indent level should be 4 spaces.

When you use continuation lines, they should align the wrapped elements using one of two methods:

- Vertically with the Python implicit way of joining lines inside braces, brackets, and parentheses, or

- With hanging indents

When you use a hanging indent, consider that there shouldn't be any arguments on line one and that, to mark the continuation line, indentation must be used.

Consider the following examples:

The Right Way:

```
# Aligned with an opening delimiter.
foo     =     long_function_name(var_four,
var_three,
                       var_two,
var_one)
```

```
# and some more indentation included so
this is distinguished from the rest of
the code

def long_function_name(
        var_four, var_three, var_two,
        var_one):
    print(var_four)

# Hanging indents should be used to add a
level.
foo = long_function_name(
    var_four, var_three,
    var_two, var_one)
```

The Wrong Way:

```
# Arguments on first line are forbidden
when you are not using vertical
alignment.
foo    =     long_function_name(var_four,
var_three,
    var_two, var_one)

# More indentation is required as the
indentation is not distinguishable from
the rest.
def long_function_name(
    var_four, var_three, var_two,
    var_one):
    print(var_four)
```

When it comes to continuation lines, the rule on 4 indent spaces is optional:

```
# it is possible for hanging indents *to*
be indented to more or less than 4
spaces.
```

```
foo = long_function_name(
  var_four, var_three,
  var_two, var_one)
```

When you use an if-statement with a long
condition that can be written over more than
one line, note that there is an easy to create a
natural indent of 4 spaces for the rest of the
lines in the conditional – use a keyword of 2
characters (for example, if) along with one
space and an opening parenthesis. However,
visually, this can look like some kind of
incompatibility with the indented code within
the if-statement, which will already have a 4-
space indent. There is no real position on
whether to distinguish these conditional lines
from the code inside the nest but there are a
few acceptable options you can use, including
but not limited to:

```
# No extra indentation used.
if (this_is_one_thing and
    that_is_something_else):
    do_this()

# Add a comment, which will provide some
help in the editors
# supporting highlighting of syntax.
if (this_is_one_thing and
    that_is_something_else):
    # as both conditions are true, we can
tweak.
    do_this()
```

```
# Add more indentation to the conditional
continuation line.
if (this_is_one_thing
        and that_is_something_else):
    do_this()
```

Now, when you have a construction of multiple lines, the closing brace, parentheses, or bracket can line up in one of two places – either beneath the beginning character that is NOT a white space on the end line of the list:

```
my_list = [
    6, 5, 4,
    3, 2, 1,
    ]
result                              =
a_function_that_will_take_arguments(
    'f', 'e', 'd',
    'c', 'b', 'a',
    )
```

Or it can be lined up beneath the beginning character of the first line in the multiple line construction:

```
my_list = [
    6, 5, 4,
    3, 2, 1,
]
result                              =
a_function_that_will_take_arguments(
    'f', 'e', 'd',
    'c', 'b', 'a',
)
```

Chapter 4: Idioms

Programming idioms are, in simple terms, the way in which Python code should be written. We often refer to idiomatic code as Pythonic code and, although there tends to be one very obvious way to write something, the actual way in which Pythonic code is written can be a bit obscure to those who are new to Python. So, you need to learn good idioms and some of the more common ones are:

Unpacking

Provided you know how long a tuple or list is, unpacking allows you to give each element a name. For example, `enumerate()` gives us a tuple with 2 elements for each of the items in the list:

```
for    the    index,    each    item    in
enumerate(this_list):
    #  do  something  with  the  index  and
each item
```

You can also use unpacking to swap the variables:

```
b, a = a, b
```

And you can use nested unpacking:

```
c, (b, a) = 3, (2, 1)
```

When Python 3 was implemented, it came with a new extended unpacking method:

```
c *the_rest = [3, 2, 1]
# c = 3, the_rest = [2, 1]
c, *the_middle, c = [4, 3, 2, 1]
# c = 4, the_middle = [3, 2], c = 1
```

Creating Ignored Variables

If you wanted to assign something but do not
need to use the variable, you would use ___. For
example:

```
filename = 'footbar.txt'
basename,        __,            ext          =
filename.rpartition('.')
```

NOTE
You will often see it recommended that you use
a single underscore (_) for variables that are
throwaway, rather than using a double
underscore(__). The problem with this is, "-",
the single underscore, tends to be used in the
`gettext()` function as an alias. It is also used to
store the value of the previous operation at the
interactive prompt. When you use a double
underscore, "__", it is clear and it is
convenient. It also cuts out the accidental risk
of interfering with the other use cases of the
single underscore.

Creating Length-N Lists

To create a length-N list that is of the same
thing, you would use the * list operator

```
four_zeros = [Zero] * 4
```

To create a length-N list of a list you should not use the * operator. That operator creates lists of N that refer to the same list and that is not what we want here. Instead, we use a list comprehension:

```
four_lists = [[] for __ in xrange(4)]
```

Note – If you are using Python 3, use **range()** and not **xrange()**

Creating Strings from Lists

The most common idiom for creating strings is **str.join()** on empty strings:

```
letters = ['c', 'l', o, 't']
word = ''.join(letters)
```

This sets a value of "clot" to the variable *word.* You can apply this idiom to tuples and lists.

Searching a Collection for an Item

On occasion, you will need to search a collection for a specific option and there are two ways to do this – using lists or sets

Look at this example:

```
s = set(['c', 'l', 'o', 't'])
l = ['c', 'l', 'o', 't']
```

```
def lookup_set(s):
    return 's' in s

def lookup_list(l):
    return 's' in l
```

Now, both of these functions look exactly the same simply because `lookup_set` uses that fact that Python sets are hash tables. However, the performance of `lookup` in each of the examples is different. In order to decide whether a specific item is contained in a list, Python has to search through every single item until it finds one that matches. This takes time, especially if you have a long list. With sets, each item has a hash that tells Python where to look for the matching item. This makes the search much quicker even if the sets are big ones. You can also search dictionaries in the same way. Because there is a difference in the performance, it is a better idea to use a set or a dictionary rather than a list in the following cases:

- Where a collection contains a lot of items

- Where you are going to be searching for items in a collection on a repeated basis

- There are no duplicate items

In cases of smaller collections or those that you are not likely to be searching on a frequent basis, the extra memory and time needed to set the hash table up will, more often than not, be more than the time you save by improving the speed of the search

Chapter 5: Comments

Because you already have some experience of Python coding, you will know that a comment is invisible when the program is run. A comment is there to help the coder and others who read it to understand what has been done and why. Now, some people think that, because they are invisible then there is no need to write them while others write comments that make no sense and that contradict their code. I have to tell you that, out of the two, having a contradictory comment is far worse than not writing one at all and, as such, whenever you make changes to your code, you must make sure that you update your comments.

When you write a comment, ensure that it is a proper sentence with a proper ending. As it is when you write anything, your comment, be it a sentence or a phrase, must have a capital letter to start it. The only exception to that rule is if it is an identifier that starts with a lower-case letter – a golden rule here is that you NEVER change the case of an identifier!

If you are using a short comment you can leave off the full-stop at the end. If you are writing block comments, these tend to be made up of at least one paragraph, sometimes more, each one built from whole sentences. Each of these sentences must have a full-stop. Following each full-stop there should be 2 spaces and all comments should be written in English. The only exception to this is if you are 200% certain that your code is never going to be read by people who do not speak or read your language

Block Comments:

A block comment tends to apply to some or all of the code that comes after it. The comment should be indented in the exact same way as the code it refers to and each line of each block must begin with a # and one space. The only exception is if you have used indented text within the comment. All paragraphs in each block comment must be separated with a line that contains one #.

Inline Comments

These should be used as little as possible. As a refresher, an inline comment is a comment that is placed on the same line that a statement is on. An inline comment has to be separated from the statement by a minimum of two spaces and they must begin with one # and one space.

In all honesty, you should avoid using inline comments because they are not really necessary and can cause an unwanted distraction.

For example, you should never do this:

```
x = x + 1                 # Increment x
```

However, sometimes, this could be useful:

```
x = x + 1                    # Compensate
for the border
```

Chapter 6:
Conventions

To make your Python code much read better, follow these conventions:

Look to see if your variables are equal to a constant. There is no need for an explicit comparison of the values to 0, None or True; instead, you could add it into the if-statement. Look at the following examples:

A Bad Example:

```
if attr == True:
    print 'True!'

if attr == None:
    print 'attr is None!'
```

A Good Example:

```
# Just look at the value
if attr:
    print 'attr is the best!'

# or check to see what the opposite is
if not attr:
    print 'attr is the worst!'

# or, as None is considered to be false,
make you sure you run an explicit check
for it
if attr is None:
    print 'attr is None!'
```

How to Access Dictionary Elements:

Instead of using the method **dict.has-key()**, use the syntax, **x in d** or use **dict.get()** to pass default arguments to.

A Bad Example:
```
d = {'hello': 'world'}
if d.has_key('hello'):
    print d['hello']    # prints 'world'
else:
    print 'the_default_value'
```

A Good Example:
```
d = {'hello': 'world'}

print  d.get('hello',  'default_value')  #
prints 'world'
print  d.get('thingy',  'default_value')  #
prints 'default_value'

# Or:
if 'hello' in d:
    print d['hello']
```

Manipulate Lists the Short Way

You don't need to be long-winded when it comes to manipulating lists; use list comprehensions or the **filter()** or **map()** functions to use concise syntax when you want to perform an operation on a list.

A Bad Example:
```
# Filter all elements that are more than
4
a = [5, 4, 3]
b = []
```

```
for i in a:
    if i > 4:
        b.append(i)
```

A Good Example:

```
a = [5, 4, 3]
b = [i for i in a if i > 4]
# Or:
b = filter(lambda x: x > 4, a)
```

Another Bad Example:

```
# Add 3 to all members f the list.
a = [5, 4, 3]
for i in range(len(a)):
    a[i] += 3
```

Another Good Example:

```
a = [5, 4, 3]
a = [i + 3 for i in a]
# Or:
a = map(lambda i: i + 3, a)
```

You can also use the function **enumerate()** to keep an account of where you are in a list:

```
a = [5, 4, 3]
for i, item in enumerate(a):
    print i, item
# prints
# 0 5
# 1 4
# 2 3
```

This function reads better than trying to manually handle a counter and it is far more optimal for iterators

Reading from a File

When you want to read from a file, it is best to use the **with open** syntax as this will close the files for you automatically.

A Bad Example:

```
f = open('file.txt')
a = f.read()
print a
f.close()
```

A Good Example:

```
with open('file.txt') as f:
    for line in f:
        print line
```

Using the **with** statement is far more efficient because it makes sure the file is always closed even when the **with** block contains an exception

Line Continuations

There are accepted limits to logical code lines and when you have one that is longer, it should be split up over several lines. Your Python interpreter will take consecutive lines and, so long as the final character on each line is a backslash (/), it will join the lines. However, although this can be useful sometimes, really you should avoid doing it because it can be fragile. If you were to add a whitespace after the backslash, it can break your code and the results might not be what you expected.

A better way to do this is to enclose elements inside parentheses. If there is an unclosed parenthesis at the end of the line, the next line will be joined, and so on until there is a closed parenthesis. You could also use square or curly braces to do the same thing, so long as you remain consistent – whatever you use to start, you must also use to finish.

A Bad Example:

```
an_incredibly_big_string = """For many
years I would go to bed early. Sometimes,
\
    after I had put out my light, my eyes
would shut so fast that I would not even
\
    have the time to say "I am going to
sleep.""""

from some.module.inside.another.module
import a_good_function,
another_good_function, \
    yet_another_good_function
```

A Good Example:

```
my_incredibly_big_string = (
    "For many years, I would go to bed
early. Sometimes, "
    "when I had put out my light, my eyes
would shut so fast "
```

```
    "that  I  would  not  even  have  time  to
say "I am going to sleep.""
)

from      some.module.inside.another.module
import (
    a_good_function,
another_good_function,
yet_another_good_function)
```

That said, if you find that you are having to
keep on splitting up long lines, it is just a sign
that you are trying to do too much and this will
affect the readability of the code

Chapter 7:
Method and
Function
Arguments

For the first argument in any instance method always use self and, for the first argument in any class method, always use cls.

If the name of a function's argument is the same as one of the reserved keywords, then it is best to add one trailing underscore than it is to use a corrupted spelling or an abbreviation. As such, you should `class_` rather than `clss`. Perhaps even better than causing a clash - use a synonym.

Function Arguments

There are 4 ways that you can pass an argument to a function:

1. **Positional Argument** – these are mandatory and do not contain any default values. The positional is the simplest argument form and are used for the arguments that are a complete part of the meaning of a function; they also have a natural order so, in the following example, the function user should find it easy to remember that the 2 functions need 2 arguments and they should remember the order:

   `Send(message,    recipient)` and
   `point(x, y)`

In both cases, you can use the argument names when you call the functions and, by doing this, you can change the order the arguments are in. For example, you could call `send(recipient='world', message='Hello')` and `point(y=2, x=1)`. However, as you can see from this, it is not very readable and there are way more words there than we need. Compare that version to the one that is more straightforward – `send('Hello', 'World')` and `point(1,2)` and you can see the difference in readability instantly.

   2. **Keyword Argument** – these do contain default values and they are not mandatory. Keyword arguments are sometimes used for optional parameters that you send to the function. When a function contains at least 2 or 3, preferably more, positional parameters, it is not easy to remember. Using a keyword argument that has a default value is more helpful. For example, you could define a complete **send** function as `send(message, to, cc=None, bcc=None)`. The use of `cc` and `bcc` is optional and both have a value of `None` if they are not given another value.

There are a few ways that you can call a function with a keyword argument in Python. For example, you could follow the argument order in a definition and no explicitly name those arguments; for example, `send('Hello', 'World', 'Galactus', 'God')`. In this, you are sending a carbon copy of the message to Galactus and a blind carbon copy to God. You can also name the arguments in a different order, for example, `send('Helloagain', 'World', bcc='God', cc='Galactus')`. Unless you have a very good reason not to follow the correct syntax as closely as possible, these two examples are best avoided; they are verbose and not readable. The best way, the way that is closest to the function definition, is `send('Hello', 'World', cc='Galactus', bcc='God')`.

3. **Arbitrary Argument List - T**his is the next way of passing an argument to a function. Sometimes, the intention of a function is better expressed with a signature that has a number of positional arguments, a number that can be extended. In that case, you are better using the `*args` constructs to define it. In the body of the argument, `args` is a tuple of all of the positional arguments that are left. For example, you can use `send(message, *args)` and list all of the recipients as a separate argument: `send('Hello', 'Galactus', 'Dad', 'God')` — in the body of the function,

`*args` is equal to (`'Galactus'`, `'Dad'`, `'God'`)

However, you should really use this construct cautiously because it does have some drawbacks. If a function is sent a list that contains arguments that are of the same or similar nature, a better definition would be a function of a single argument; that single argument would be a sequence or a list. For example, if `send` had several recipients, you would be better with an explicit definition: `send('Hello', 'God', 'Dad', 'Galactus')` and then call it by using `send('Hello',['God', 'Dad', 'Galactus'])`. In this way, the function user can change the recipient list beforehand and that opens up the possibility for any sequence that can't be unpacked to be passed, and that includes iterators.

4. **Arbitrary Keyword Argument Dictionary** - This is final way of passing an argument to a function. If a function needs an unknown array of named arguments, you can use the construct `**kwargs`. Within the body of the function, ****kwargs** is a dictionary that contains all of the named arguments that have been passed and not caught by another keyword argument in the signature of the function

However, you should use the same level of caution that you did with arbitrary argument lists, for pretty much the same reasons. These are powerful techniques that should only be used when you can prove that it is necessary to use them. They most definitely should not be used if there is a clearer and simpler construct that will do the job.

It really is down to you, the programmer, to decide which of the function arguments are optional keywords and which are positional and to determine whether you should use the more advanced techniques to pass the arguments.

Keep it simple and follow these rules of writing Python functions that:

- Are readable – the names and the arguments do not need any explanations

- Are easily changeable – you can add a keyword argument in without the rest of the code breaking.

Chapter 8: Naming Conventions

To be honest, the Python library naming conventions are something of a mess so we are never going to be totally consistent. However, there are some naming standards that are recommended and all new packages and modules, and that includes any third-party frameworks, must be written to these standards. That said, if you are using an existing library with a different style, stick to that style because consistency is preferable, especially in terms of readability

The first and most important principle to learn is that, where you are using names that are a visible part of a public API, you must use a convention that reflects that usage of the name, rather than the implementation of it.

Descriptive

There are quite a few different naming styles so it is helpful to recognize which one is in use, independently of the usage. These are the most commonly distinguished naming styles:

- `B` – single uppercase
- `b` – single lowercase
- `lowercase_with_underscores`
- `lowercase`
- `UPPERCASE_WITH_UNDERSCORES`
- `UPPERCASE`

- `CapitalizedWords` – often called CamelCase because the letters look somewhat bumpy*
- `mixedCase` – different from CamelCase because the first letter is in lowercase
- `Capital_Words_With_Underscore` - not a pretty style!

* When you use abbreviations in CamelCase, you should make sure all of the abbreviation letters are capitalized. For example, rather than using `HttpServerError`, use `HTTPServerError` instead

You can also use another style, that of putting a unique prefix, a short one, that puts a group of related names together. This doesn't get used very much in Python but I mention it just so that you know it is there. An example would be the function `os.stat()` - this will return a tuple that contains items that have names like `st_size`, `st_mode`, `st_mtime` and so on.

These are some of the forms that use a trailing or a leading underscore and can usually be combined with any of the case conventions:

- `_one_leading_underscore` - this is generally an indicator of "internal use" that is not very strong.

- `One_trailing_underscore_` - generally used to stop a conflict with a Python keyword, for example: `Apinter.Toplevel(master,class_='ClassName")`

- `__two_leading_underscores` – when you name a class attribute, this invokes mangling of a name, for example: `(inside class FootBar, __boo)` would become `(_FootBar__boo)`

- `__two_leading_and_two_trailing_underscores` are attributes or "magic" objects that reside in a namespace that is user-controlled. For example: `__init__`, `__file__`, or `__import__`.

Prescriptive

These are the names you should avoid:

Never use 'O' (uppercase oh), 'l' (lowercase el) or 'I' (uppercase eye) when you are writing variable names of a single character. Depending on what font you are using, these may be, these can be confused with the numbers 'o' and '1' – if you do find yourself thinking about using 'l', use the uppercase 'L' instead.

Names for Modules and Packages

All module names should be short and lowercase. You can use an underscore in a module name but only if it makes it more readable. The same goes for Python packages – short and lowercase names – but don't use underscores.

Where you have an extension module that has been written in C or in C++ and it is accompanied by a Python module that has an interface that is more object-oriented, the C or C++ module will have a leading underscore, for example, `_socket`

Class Names

Class names usually use the CapWords or CamelCase convention.

Built-in names have their own separate convention and are usually a single word or 2 words in one, for example, `'Hello'` or `'HelloWorld`. The CamelCase convention tends to be kept for built-in constants and for exception names.

Type Variables

The names of the type variables usually use CamelCase and short names are preferred, for example, `Num`, `AnyStr`. You should add a suffix (_co or _contra) to the variables to declare contravariant or covariant behavior. For example:

```
Import TypeVar
```

Would become

```
VT_co = TypeVar('VT_co', covariant=True)
KT_contra = TypeVar('KT_contra',
contravariant=True)
```

Names of Exceptions

Exceptions are classes and, as such, you should use the class convention for naming. That said, if the exception is an error, make sure that you use the 'Error' suffix on the name.

Global Variables

Provided the variable is used inside a single module, the naming conventions are the same as for naming functions.

Functions

All function names are in lowercase and the words are separated by an underscore where needed to make it more readable. mixedCase conventions are only to be used in the context where this is already the style in order to keep backward compatibility intact.

Instance Variables and Method Names

Again, the naming conventions for functions apply here – using lowercase with intermittent underscores. If you are using an instance variable or a non-public method, you should use a single leading underscore. To stop a name from clashing with a subclass, two leading underscores should be used as a way of invoking the name mangling rules in Python.

When these rules are invoked, the name is mangled with the class name. For example, class Foo contains an attribute called `__a`. This cannot be accessed using `Foo.__a`. As a rule, you should only use a double leading underscore when the name is likely to come into conflict with class attributes that are designed as subclasses.

Constants

These tend to be defined on module level and are all uppercase with separating underscores, for example, `MAX_OVERFLOW`

Inheritance Design

One rule to abide by is to determine if the instance variable or class method is non-public or public. If you can't decide, go for non-public as you can easily change it to public later on, whereas changing public to non-public is not so easy.

A public attribute is one that clients that are not related to the class would use while a non-public attribute is one that is not intended for use by a third-party. With a public attribute, you guarantee backward compatibility from start to finish while, with the non-pubic attribute you do not and can remove or make changes to the attribute. Note that the term "private" is not used and this is because there is no real private attribute in the Python language.

One other attribute category is that which is a protected attribute. In Python, they come under the subclass API. There are those classes that are designed solely as classes to inherit from, whether it is as a way of extending or modifying certain aspects of the behavior. When you design a class like this, always make sure that you make explicit decisions about the attributes – are they public, only to be used by the base class or are they in the subclass API?

With all of this, these are the Pythonic guidelines:

- A public attribute must not have a leading underscore

- If a public attribute clashes with a keyword (reserved), add one trailing underscore to the attribute name. This is the preferred method over using a corruption in spelling or an abbreviation.

- With a public data attribute, the best way is to expose only the name of the attribute, without using any complicated mutator or accessor methods. If a simple attribute needs to expand its functional behavior, Python makes it easy.

- If you are using a class that is going to be subclassed and you are also using attributes that are not going to be subclassed, think about adding 2 leading underscores but do not add in any trailing underscores. This will invoke name mangling and helps to lower the risk of name clashes if the subclasses have attributes with the same name in them.

Chapter 9: Using Whitespace in Statements and Expressions

First, some of the peeves about whitespaces:

Do not use unnecessary whitespaces in these cases:

- Immediately within braces, brackets or parentheses

A Good Example:
```
ham(spam[1], {eggs: 2})
```

A Bad Example:
```
ham( spam[ 1 ], { eggs: 2 } )
```

- Immediately in front of a colon, semicolon or a comma:

A Good Example:
```
if x == 4: print x, y; x, y = y, x
```

A Bad Example:
```
if x == 4 : print x , y ; x , y = y , x
```

However, where you have a slice, the colon is similar to a binary operator and it should contain an equal amount on each side. Where you have an extended slice, both of the colons must contain the exact same level of spacing. The exception to this is a slice parameter that has been omitted, along with the space.

A Good Example:
```
spam[1:8], spam[1:8:2], spam[:8:2],
spam[1::2], spam[1:8:]
```

```
spam[lower:upper], spam[lower:upper:],
spam[lower::step]
spam[lower+offset : upper+offset]
spam[: upper_fn(x) : step_fn(x)], ham[::
step_fn(x)]
spam[lower + offset : upper + offset]
```

A Bad Example:
```
spam[lower + offset:upper + offset]
spam[1: 8], ham[1 :8], ham[1:8 :2]
spam[lower : : upper]
spam[ : upper]
```

- Right before the opening parenthesis that begins the argument list of the function call:

A Good Example:
```
ham(1)
```

A Bad Example:
```
ham (1)
```

- Right in front of the open parenthesis that starts a slicing or an indexing:

A Good Example:
```
dct['key'] = lst[index]
```

A Bad Example:
```
dct ['key'] = lst [index]
```

- When there is more than a single space around an operator, such as an assignment, that aligns it with another operator

A Good Example:
```
x = 1
y = 2
long_variable = 3
```

A Bad Example:
```
x             = 1
y             = 2
long_variable = 3
```

Other Recommendations

Avoid having trailing whitespace throughout your code because it is not visible and it can cause confusion. For example, if you put in a backslash and follow it with a space and then a newline – this would not be counted as a line continuation. In fact, some text editors will not preserve it and there are projects that contain pre-commit hooks that will simply reject it – one of those is CPython.

The following binary operators should be surrounded by single spaces – one on each side:

- assignment (=)
- augmented assignment (+=, = etc.)

The following comparisons are treated the same:

- ==

- <
- >
- !=
- <>
- <=
- >=
- in
- not in
- is
- is not

And these Booleans:

- and
- or
- not

If you use operators that have different priorities, think about putting whitespace around the lowest priority operators – use your best judgment here. However, you should not use any more than a single space and make sure that each side of the operator has the same amount of whitespace – don't put 1 on one side and 2 on the other:

A Good Example:

```
i = i + 1
submitted += 1
x = x*2 - 1
hypot2 = x*x + y*y
c = (a+b) * (a-b)
```

A Bad Example:

```
i=i+1
submitted +=1
x = x * 2 - 1
hypot2 = x * x + y * y
c = (a + b) * (a - b)
```

When you use an = sign to indicate default values for parameters or keyword arguments, do not use whitespace around the sign:

A Good Example:

```
def complex(real, imag=0.0):
    return magic(r=real, i=imag)
```

A Bad Example:

```
def complex(real, imag = 0.0):
    return magic(r = real, i = imag)
```

Use the standard rules for colons with function annotations and make sure there are spaces surrounding the -> if it is used:

A Good Example:

```
def munge(input: AnyStr): ...
def munge() -> AnyStr: ...
```

A Bad Example:

```
def munge(input:AnyStr): ...
def munge()->PosInt: ...
```

When you combine a default value and an argument annotation, spaces should surround the = sign – do not do this unless the argument has both the default and the annotation:

A Good Example:
```
def munge(sep: AnyStr = None): ...
def munge(input: AnyStr, sep: AnyStr =
None, limit=1000): ...
```

A Bad Example:
```
def munge(input: AnyStr=None): ...
def munge(input: AnyStr, limit = 1000):
...
```

It is not good practice to use compound statements – several statements on one line:

A Good Example:
```
if foo == 'that':
    do_that_thing()
do_one()
do_two()
do_three()
```

Best Not to Do:
```
if foo == 'that': do_that_thing()
do_one(); do_two(); do_three()
```

It is, on occasion, alright to use an if, for and while statement on one line, provided they have small bodies but you should never do this for statements that have several clauses. Also, never fold really long lines:

Best Not to Do:

```
if foo == 'that': do_that_thing()
for x in lst: total += x
while t < 10: t = delay()
```

Most Definitely Not:

```
if foo == 'that': do_that_thing()
else: do_non_that_thing()

try: something()
finally: cleanup()

do_one();      do_two();      do_three(long,
argument,
                              list,    like,
this)

if foo == 'that': one(); two(); three()
```

Conclusion

Thank you once again for reading my book, I truly hope that it was able to help you understand how to write more effective and efficient Python code.

From here, the next step is to, quite simply, practice. The more you do, the better you will get and, eventually, you will be writing Python code like a pro! Research, join online Python forums and join the Python community to learn more and to advance your skills.

Lastly, if you found this book helpful, please can I ask a small favor of you? Please consider leaving a review for me at Amamzon.com; it isn't only helpful to me, it also benefits prospective readers

Thank you and good luck on your journey to becoming a better Python programmer

About the Author

Charlie Masterson is a computer programmer and instructor who have developed several applications and computer programs.

As a computer science student, he got interested in programming early but got frustrated learning the highly complex subject matter.
Charlie wanted a teaching method that he could easily learn from and develop his programming skills. He soon discovered a teaching series that made him learn faster and better.

Applying the same approach, Charlie successfully learned different programming languages and is now teaching the subject matter through writing books.
With the books that he writes on computer programming, he hopes to provide great value and help readers interested to learn computer-related topics.

www.ingramcontent.com/pod-product-compliance
Lightning Source LLC
Chambersburg PA
CBHW061033050326
40689CB00012B/2792